WHEN THIS
CRUEL
WAR
IS OVER

WHEN THIS
CRUEL
WAR
IS OVER

THE CIVIL WAR
HOME FRONT

Duane Damon

Lerner Publications Company • Minneapolis

To Sarah and Andrew, with love

Front cover: A family at a Union encampment near Washington, D.C. Women and children occasionally followed their husbands and fathers to war. In camp, women cooked for the soldiers, did laundry, nursed the sick, and taught men to read.

Page 2: In Leaving Home, *by William Gilbert Gaul, a young Confederate bids his family farewell.*

Copyright © 1996 by Duane Damon

Library of Congress Cataloging-in-Publication Data

Damon, Duane.
    When this cruel war is over : the Civil War home front / Duane Damon.
      p. cm.
    ISBN 0–8225–1731–0 (alk. paper)
    1. United States—History—Civil War, 1861–1865—Juvenile literature.
  I. Title.
    E468.D36 1996
    973.7'1—dc20   95-11740

Manufactured in the United States of America
1 2 3 4 5 6 - JR - 01 00 99 98 97 96

Contents

THE TRUMPET OF WAR

War seems inevitable, and while I am trying to employ the passing hour, a cloud hangs over us and all that surrounds us.

—Judith McGuire, Alexandria, Virginia, 1861

CHARLESTON

MERCURY

EXTRA:

Passed unanimously at 1.15 o'clock, P. M. December 20th, 1860.

AN ORDINANCE

To dissolve the Union between the State of South Carolina and other States united with her under the compact entitled " The Constitution of the United States of America."

We, the People of the State of South Carolina, in Convention assembled, do declare and ordain, and it is hereby declared and ordained.

That the Ordinance adopted by us in Convention, on the twenty-third day of May, in the year of our Lord one thousand seven hundred and eighty-eight, whereby the Constitution of the United States of America was ratified, and also, all Acts and parts of Acts of the General Assembly of this State, ratifying amendments of the said Constitution, are hereby repealed; and that the union now subsisting between South Carolina and other States, under the name of " The United States of America," is hereby dissolved.

THE

UNION

IS

DISSOLVED!

In the inky blackness of a South Carolina night, a small boat made its way across Charleston Harbor. Ahead lay the five-sided silhouette of Fort Sumter. There, Major Robert Anderson and a command of 68 Union soldiers and eight officers had been holed up for three and a half months. Surrounding Anderson's lonely position was a force of 6,000 Confederate, or Rebel, troops, led by Brigadier General Pierre G. T. Beauregard. The two commanders were not strangers. Anderson had been Beauregard's artillery instructor at West Point, the United States Military Academy, some 25 years before.

Aboard the boat were four representatives of the Confederate States of America. Among them was a former U.S. senator, Colonel James

Chesnut Jr. Courteously, but grimly, the Confederates informed Anderson that he must surrender the fort. If he failed to do so by 4:00 A.M., the representatives warned, the Rebel batteries would open fire. Anderson refused.

Across the harbor, James Chesnut's wife tensely awaited the outcome. A nearby church bell tolled the appointed hour. "I count four—St. Michael chimes," Mary Chesnut wrote. "I begin to hope. At half past four, the heavy booming of the cannon. I sprang out of bed. And on my knees . . . I prayed as I never prayed before."

Confederate artillery splashed a spectacular display in the sky over Sumter. Thirty-four grueling hours later, Major Anderson surrendered.

As Confederates opened fire on Fort Sumter, nearby Charleston residents looked on from their rooftops. The Civil War had begun.

No one had been killed in the bombardment, but its importance was unmistakable. As of April 12, 1861, North—the Union—was at war with South—the Confederacy.

DIVIDED LOYALTIES

Long before Confederate guns boomed over Sumter, America had already begun its Civil War. What ended as a clash of great armies started as a battle of ideas and economies. It was a conflict of secession against union, slavery against freedom, farm against factory. Some people would say the war was a struggle of the nation's past against its future.

For decades, the enslavement of black Americans had been a sore spot in relations between the North and South. By the mid-1800s, most Northern states had outlawed slavery. Northern blacks lived as free people—although in most cases their rights were severely limited. But Southern blacks were almost all slaves, and white Southerners jealously guarded their "right" to own them. Slave labor helped Southern farms and plantations prosper.

Field hands plant sweet potatoes on Edisto Island, South Carolina, 1862.

As new western territories joined the United States, Northerners grew wary that slavery would spread. Many Northern politicians wanted to abolish slavery, or at least limit it to those areas where it was already practiced. Southerners opposed any restrictions on slavery. Several Southern states threatened to secede—or withdraw—from the Union if the right to own slaves was ever denied.

Few people felt the terrible tug-of-war between North and South as keenly as John J. Crittenden of Kentucky. Throughout 1860, the aging statesman pleaded in the U.S. Senate for "peace and harmony and union." While his Southern colleagues thundered and roared against the North, Crittenden's home state teetered on the brink of secession. Desperately, he held out the olive branch of compromise. He proposed a plan that would protect the practice of slavery in certain states if the South promised not to leave the Union. But the Senate refused even to bring the Crittenden Compromise to a vote.

In the meantime, Crittenden's two sons chose up sides. Thomas Crittenden became a major general in the Union army. His brother George donned the gray uniform of a Confederate officer.

In some places, entire communities had mixed loyalties. The state of Missouri supplied the Union army with 22 regiments at the siege of Vicksburg. The same state dispatched 17 regiments to fight for the Confederates. Through four long years of agonizing warfare, conflicting beliefs would continue to divide the United States and its people.

BATTLING ECONOMIES

In 1861, the North and South were much like two separate and distinct countries. With 90 percent of the nation's factories, the North was an industrial powerhouse. Massachusetts alone produced one-and-a-half times as many goods as the entire Confederacy. From the fertile farmlands of the Midwest came enough grain to feed the North with huge amounts left over for export to Europe. The North's population of 20 million people in 23 states was more than double that of the South.

Their very lifestyles put the soon-to-be Confederates at a serious disadvantage. Theirs was an agricultural society, not an industrial one. The

At a wharf in Charleston, cotton is readied for shipment to American and European ports.

South enjoyed a wealth of raw materials but was poor in factories, skilled labor, and machinery. The region's economy rested on the sale of its major crops—particularly cotton—to countries across the Atlantic Ocean.

To make matters more difficult, more than one-third of the South's nine million people were black slaves. At first this ratio benefited the plantation owners and farmers of the Confederacy. Since only white men were allowed to serve in the Southern army, slaves stayed at home to work the fields. But as the war dragged on and Confederate forces dwindled, the South would sorely miss this neglected source of military manpower.

All of these differences meant that the North was better prepared to wage war than the South. By the time war broke out, smoke-belching

Foundries and factories in the North quickly produced the machinery of war.

factories in Northern states were already turning out an impressive array of labor-saving machines for the farm. Mowers, reapers, harrows, threshers, and cultivators allowed Northerners to maintain their farms with fewer hands than ever before. Gearing up to manufacture rifles, cannon, ammunition, and uniforms would be a fairly simple matter.

The South, on the other hand, clung stubbornly to its old methods and traditions. "When the war began," wrote historian Bruce Catton in *The Civil War,* "the Confederacy had almost nothing but men. The men were as good as the very best, but their country simply could not support them." To meet the needs of its armies, the South was forced to switch from its century-old economy based on cotton production to one based on manufacturing. It was a nearly impossible task.

Adding to these woes was the sorry state of the South's transportation system. In all of the Confederacy there were only 9,000 miles of railroad track, and much of that was in poor repair. By comparison, the North boasted some 22,000 miles of track. Producing enough goods in the Southern states would become difficult. Moving these goods from factory or farm to consumers would become a nightmare.

Outnumbered, outgunned, and outmanned, the South entered the conflict as determined as the North was confident. But while the North's economy would thrive on the demands of war, the South's economy was fated to be crushed by them.

THE FUSE AND THE MATCH

In the 1840s and 1850s, as an uneasy South eyed the growing wealth and power of the North, the debate over slavery neared the boiling point. In Congress, a parade of proposals and compromises aimed to soothe the rising tensions. Some proposals only heated passions even more. The Fugitive Slave Act, a provision of the Compromise of 1850, guaranteed that slaves who escaped to Northern states could be returned to their Southern masters. This unpopular act enraged many Northerners, who flocked to the banner of abolition, the movement to end slavery. A new proposal in 1854 fanned the flames still hotter. The Kansas-Nebraska Act allowed the settlers of these two territories to decide whether to enter the Union as slave states or free states. In Illinois, this act roused a successful lawyer and former congressman to leave private life and return to politics. His name was Abraham Lincoln.

The conflict took a dramatic turn in October 1859. Descending on the Virginia town of Harpers Ferry, a gaunt, fiery-eyed abolitionist named John Brown and a loyal band of his followers stormed the government arsenal there. Brown hoped to furnish arms to slaves, who would then rise up against their owners. The strategy was ambitious—and doomed. Government troops attacked and killed 10 of his men. Brown himself was captured, tried for treason, and hanged.

Overnight, John Brown became a martyr to the armies of abolition. Many Northerners were shocked by his violent methods, but they

John Brown hoped to lead slaves in rebellion.

cheered his intentions. The essayist Henry David Thoreau hailed Brown as "an angel of light."

The Harpers Ferry raid stunned the South. Many slave owners feared murderous revolts, in which slaves would burn plantations and slaughter their masters in their beds. For many Southerners, the raid on Harpers Ferry was the last straw. "The day of compromise is passed," swore an editorial in a Charleston newspaper, " . . . there is no peace for the South in the Union."

Anxious Southerners turned their eyes toward the 1860 presidential election, now just months away. Of particular concern was a man who had once said, "A house divided against itself cannot stand. The nation cannot endure permanently half-slave and half-free."

Unfortunately for Southern hopes, this was the very candidate the six-year-old Republican Party nominated. Like his party, Abraham Lincoln was committed to stopping the spread of slavery. "Wrong as we think slavery is, we can yet afford to let it alone where it is," he said in a campaign speech in New York. "But can we . . . allow it to spread into the National Territories, and overrun us here in the Free States?"

Alarmed by the threat to its slave-holding interests, South Carolina vowed to leave the Union if Lincoln became president. On November 6, 1860, Lincoln was elected. Six weeks later, South Carolinian lawmakers met in Charleston and voted unanimously for secession. Within a month, Mississippi, Florida, Alabama, Georgia, and Louisiana followed suit. Texas soon joined them.

A Virginia newspaper left no doubt as to the South's opinion of the new U.S. president. Lincoln's election, growled the Richmond *Whig,* "is undoubtedly the greatest evil that has ever befallen this country."

THE CONFLICT IGNITES

James Chesnut Jr. of South Carolina became the first U.S. senator to give up his seat in Washington in support of the renegade South. On February 18, 1861, his wife, Mary, wrote in her journal: "The Southern Confederacy must be supported by calm determination and cool brains. We have risked all, and we must play our best, for the stake is life and death."

On the same day in Montgomery, Alabama, the Chesnuts' friend Jefferson Davis was sworn in as provisional president of the Confederate States of America. Davis took an unyielding stand on secession. "Governments rest on the consent of the governed," he insisted in his inaugural address. "It is the right of the people to alter or abolish them at will."

At his own inauguration, Abraham Lincoln made an eloquent appeal to the South for peace. "In *your* hands, my dissatisfied countrymen, and not *mine,* is the momentous issue of civil war. . . . We are not enemies, but friends. We must not be enemies."

But the "secesh" steamroller would not be stopped. In many Southern cities, secession was greeted with joy, public celebrations, and parades. Yet not every Southerner favored making the break. "I don't believe in

Two presidents at war: Abraham Lincoln (top) and Jefferson Davis (bottom). Shortly after Lincoln's election, Southern states withdrew from the Union, forming the Confederate States of America and naming Davis as their president.

secession, but I do in Liberty," wrote young Sarah Morgan of Baton Rouge. "I want the South to conquer, dictate its own terms, and go back into the Union."

Still, the majority of Southerners welcomed the split with the North. While the fledgling Confederate government lumbered into motion, a kind of military fever swept the South. In her diary, Kate Stone of Louisiana expressed the rising clamor for action: "Throughout the length and breadth of the land, the trumpet of war is sounding. From every hamlet and village, from city and country, men are rushing by the thousands, eager to be led in battle against Lincoln's hordes."

The fall of Fort Sumter brought prompt action from Washington. A determined President Lincoln quickly called for 75,000 volunteers to

Maine infantrymen on parade

Soldiers of the First Virginia Militia— known as the Richmond Grays

take up arms. The response was swift and spirited. The governor of Ohio had aimed at raising 13 regiments for the Union. But so great was his state's enthusiasm that he ended up with 20 regiments. "The lion in us is thoroughly roused," he announced proudly.

Virginia, Arkansas, North Carolina, and Tennessee answered Lincoln's call by angrily pulling out of the Union. In all parts of the South, Confederate volunteers were cheered by friends and family as shining knights destined to save their homeland. "How we idolized our boys in gray, with their glittering guns and swords," recalled Annie Coulson Harper of Natchez, Mississippi. "Already we deemed them invincible." Only 21 at the time, Harper was stirred by the spectacle of the departing troops:

One lovely Sabbath afternoon I saw the Adams Light
Guards 200 strong . . . march down to the riverside to take
the boat which bore most of them away forever. They stood
in line from the top of the hill to the steamboat landing.
Carriages filled with grief-stricken women, mothers, sweethearts, and wives, pressed closely as possible to the ranks,
returning the last fond look of love which left them so
despairing. At last the word was given: Forward march! And
they filed on board with colors flying, drums beating, bands
playing, cannon firing—hurrahing and waving until in the
distance they faded away.

The zeal for battle was not limited to white Americans. In a show of
patriotism and sympathy for Southern slaves, many Northern black men
volunteered for service in the Union army. But these would-be soldiers
were in for a rude shock: white military leaders wanted no help from
black volunteers. For the next year and a half, blacks who wanted to take
up arms against the Confederacy were barred from joining the "white
man's war."

In the hectic and heady weeks that followed Sumter, governments and
armies North and South scrambled to prepare for their noble "adven-
ture." Few people expected the war to last more than a few months. But
a single line in the *New York Times* published two days after the opening
guns in Charleston Harbor came closer to the mark: "The curtain has
fallen upon the first act of the great tragedy of our age."

Opposite: Union recruiting poster

REAP THE WHIRLWIND

Our National Sin has found us out. . . . We have sown the wind, only to reap the whirlwind.

   —Frederick Douglass on slavery and the war, 1861

Some 35 years after the Civil War, black educator Booker T. Washington recalled what the coming conflict had meant to Southern slaves. "Even the most ignorant members of my race . . ." he recorded, "felt in their hearts that the freedom of the slaves would be the one great result of the war."

It was not easy to be optimistic. From the day in 1619 when a Dutch ship docked at Jamestown, Virginia, with 20 captive Africans aboard, slavery had been part of American life. Over the years, the "peculiar institution" died out in the North. But the South was not ready to give up the army of slaves it used to tend its millions of acres of cotton, rice, sugar, and tobacco. Then, in 1793, a Yankee (Northern) inventor named Eli Whitney gave slave owners one more reason not to.

Whitney's cotton engine, or "gin," could clean up to 1,000 pounds of cotton in a single day. Southern planters bought thousands of African slaves to keep the hungry gins fed. Although the slave trade was abolished in 1808, the American slave population grew as Africans were imported illegally and as slaves had children. By the start of the Civil War, the number of black men, women, and children in bondage had soared to four million. "Cotton is King," a South Carolina senator summed up, "and the African must be a slave."

The hardships of a slave's life were immense. Slaves had no rights. They were forbidden to vote or to own property. Teaching slaves to read and write was illegal. Some learned anyway, but 90 percent were illiterate. Slaves could neither marry nor leave their masters' property without permission. Perhaps cruelest of all, slave owners were free to sell any slave at any time to almost anyone. The auction block gave many black families their last glimpse of mothers and fathers, sons and daughters, husbands and wives.

This 19th-century lithograph shows hardworking slaves with a cotton gin and prosperous white planters inspecting their product.

TO BE SOLD & LET

BY PUBLIC AUCTION,

On *MONDAY* the 18th of *MAY*, 1829,

UNDER THE TREES.

FOR SALE,

THE THREE FOLLOWING

SLAVES,

VIZ.

HANNIBAL, about 30 Years old, an excellent House Servant, of Good Character.
WILLIAM, about 35 Years old, a Labourer.
NANCY, an excellent House Servant and Nurse.

The MEN belonging to "LEECH'S" Estate, and the WOMAN to Mrs. D. SMIT

TO BE LET,

On the usual conditions of the Hirer finding them in Food, Clot and Medical

THE FOLLOWING

MALE and FEMALE

SLAVES,

OF GOOD CHARACTERS.

ROBERT BAGLEY, about 20 Years old, a good House Servant.
WILLIAM BAGLEY, about 18 Years old, a Labourer.
JOHN ARMS, about 16 Years old.
JACK ANTONIA, about 40 Years old, a Labourer.
PHILIP, an Excellent Fisherman.
HARRY, about 27 Years old, a good House Servant.
LUCY, a Young Woman of good Character, used to House Work and the Nursery.
ELIZA, an Excellent Washerwoman.
CLARA, an Excellent Washerwoman.
FANNY, about 14 Years old, House Servant.
SARAH, about 14 Years old, House Servant.

Also for Sale, at Eleven o'Clock,

Fine Rice, Gram, Paddy, Books, Muslins, Needles, Pins, Ribbons, &c. &c.

AT ONE O'CLOCK, THAT CELEBRATED ENGLISH HORSE

BLUCHER,

Solomon Northrup, a free black man who had spent 12 years in slavery, described a day on a Louisiana plantation:

> The hands were required to be in the cotton fields as soon as it is light in the morning. . . . With the exception of ten or fifteen minutes, which is given them at noon to swallow their allowance of cold bacon, they are not permitted to be a moment idle until it is too dark to see. . . . When the moon is full, they often times labor till the middle of the night.

If a slave failed to pick the required amount of cotton, he or she could expect to be punished, often brutally. Even a minor offense might earn a slave an encounter with the lash. "A mere look, word, or motion . . . are all matters for which a slave might be whipped at any time," wrote one former slave. Not every slaveholder was this barbaric. But an existence of hopelessness and despair was the fate of most blacks in bondage.

A quarter million black people in the South didn't wear chains or live in slave quarters. These blacks had their freedom, but not much else. Like the slaves, they had no schooling and were not allowed to vote. Some free blacks managed to become educated and wealthy, but they were the exception, not the rule.

The lives of the 225,000 black Northerners were somewhat better. The New England states allowed black children to attend public schools with white youngsters. But in most ways, society in the Northern states was segregated—blacks were not permitted to mix with whites. Black people were forbidden to eat next to whites in most restaurants or to sit with them on many trains and streetcars. Only in four states did black men even enjoy the right to vote.

STRIKING A BLOW

The war's opening guns signaled little change for most slaves. When white masters left their plantations and farms to join the Confederate army, they often placed white overseers in charge. The slaves left behind were expected to do one thing: conduct business as usual. Most of the time, they did it. The majority of slaves continued working on their masters' estates for the rest of the war.

As the fighting heated up, however, outnumbered Rebel armies drew on slave labor for temporary help. Some slaves were forced to work as cooks, water bearers, and construction workers for the Southern forces. Others followed their masters into army camps as body servants. Still other slaves got even closer to the action. Virginia slave John King was pressed into service in a Confederate battery at Bull Run, Virginia:

> My work was to hand the [cannon] balls and swab out the cannon. . . . The balls from the Yankee guns fell thick all around. . . . I felt bad all the time, and thought that every minute my time would come. . . . We wished to our hearts that the Yankees would whip, and we would have run over to their side. But our officers would've shot us if we had made the attempt.

Several black men, including a banjo player, number among the sailors aboard the Union gunboat **Hunchback.**

Willingly or not, slaves also aided the Rebel cause by working in Southern factories and on railroads.

As the invading Union armies pushed farther into the South, many slaves smelled liberty. Union lines were now temptingly close, and slaves began to risk escape. A month after the firing on Fort Sumter, a small group of escaped slaves straggled into the Union camp of General Ben Butler near Norfolk, Virginia. Butler's dilemma was clear: should these fugitives be returned to their masters or be allowed to remain free? He did not debate for long. Declaring the slaves to be property seized from the enemy, he labeled them "contrabands" and put them to work as laborers in his army. Before the end of the war, more than one-half million blacks would become contrabands.

Even black people who remained in slavery found ways to serve the Union side. For Yankee soldiers escaping from Confederate prisons, the face of mercy was often black. Lieutenant Hannibal Johnson recounted his flight from a South Carolina prison camp with three fellow officers in late 1864:

> At night we approached a negro cabin for the first time; we did it with fear and trembling, but we must have food and help. Found a family of trusty negroes...who gave us a good supper, such as we had not had for many long months. . . . Here we remained until morning, when we were taken to the woods and hid there to wait for a guide which these negroes say they would furnish at dark.

For two and a half months, generous slaves aided Johnson in his return to Union lines. "If such kindness will not make one an Abolitionist," he gratefully wrote, "then his heart must be made of stone."

Sometimes nerve and good timing enabled a slave to strike a more daring blow for the Union, and for himself. In the spring of 1862, Robert Smalls was a 23-year-old slave and pilot for the Confederate steamer *Planter,* based in Charleston Harbor. From the steamer's deck, Smalls eyed the distant line of Union ships blockading the harbor and devised a bold scheme.

On the evening of May 12, the *Planter's* white officers went ashore to attend a social event. Smalls and eight black shipmates seized their chance and started the steamer's engines. Stopping only to pick up their wives and children, they steamed out across the harbor. But before they could reach the Union fleet and freedom, they had to run a deadly maze of Confederate batteries above the water and naval mines below.

Decked out in the captain's coat and straw hat, Smalls coolly gave the proper identifying signals on the steamer's whistle. No one in six unsuspecting forts so much as challenged the *Planter*. Then, running a white sheet up the vessel's flagstaff, Smalls steered his boat underneath the guns of the nearest Yankee ship—the *Onward*. "Good morning, sir!" he called to the captain. "I've brought you some of the old United States guns, sir!" With that greeting he made the *Onward* a gift of the *Planter's* cargo of four cannon and 200 pounds of ammunition.

WHITE HAND, BLACK HAND

In late 1861, Union forces took control of the Sea Islands off the South Carolina coast. Panicked whites fled, leaving behind more than 8,000 slaves. These people were soon joined by thousands of runaway slaves, most of them hungry, ill, and unschooled.

In the North, concerned blacks and whites banded together to form freedmen's aid societies. They collected clothing, medicine, and money for the former slaves. Early in 1862, teachers were dispatched southward by the dozens. Among those sent to the Sea Islands was a free black woman named Charlotte Forten. "I never before saw children so eager to learn," she wrote. "Coming to school is a constant delight and recreation to them. . . . The older ones, during the summer, work in the fields from early morning until eleven or twelve o'clock, and then come into school . . . as bright and anxious to learn as ever." At least 200,000 students attended schools set up by freedmen's aid societies during the war.

But as the North held out a helping hand to some blacks, it turned its back on others. Well into the war, the U.S. Army still refused to admit black men into its ranks. Frederick Douglass, a black editor, abolitionist, and lecturer, was one of many who challenged this policy.

For months Douglass besieged the Lincoln administration with appeals for enlisting black soldiers. "Why does the Government reject the Negro?" he demanded. "This is no time to fight with only your white hand, and allow your black hand to remain tied."

Finally, in November 1862, the first black regiment was mustered on the Sea Islands in South Carolina. Next, Massachusetts raised two black regiments, the 54th and the 55th. Douglass's sons Charles and Lewis quickly enlisted. They were in the ranks of the 54th Massachusetts when it made its famed assault on Fort Wagner, South Carolina, in July 1863.

Kate Foote of the New England Freedman's Aid Society teaches reading to former slaves in South Carolina, 1862.

An estimated 190,000 black men, many of them former slaves, saw action in the Union army. The Confederacy, on the other hand, did not enlist black men until 1865. By then the war was almost over.

ABOLITION AND JUBILEE

"Of what was John Brown convicted?" the man on the platform asked his Boston audience on the night of Brown's execution. "It was the trial of the lamb by the wolf—nothing less."

The speaker was not a campaigning politician or a fire-and-brimstone preacher. He was a mild-mannered, bespectacled husband and father named William Lloyd Garrison. His weekly newspaper, the *Liberator,* founded in 1831, was the most outspoken antislavery publication in the nation. Garrison's beliefs were unpopular and his enemies were many. He had once been attacked on a Boston street by a proslavery mob and was nearly killed. The Georgia legislature offered a $5,000 reward for his capture.

Garrison was one of hundreds of abolitionists who risked public hostility to spread their "gospel." Others were Wendell Phillips, Sarah and Angelina Grimké, Abby Kelley Foster, and Lucretia Mott. As committed as they were, not all abolitionists agreed on the best way to achieve their

Abolitionist William Lloyd Garrison

goal. Some spoke out for immediate freedom for the slaves. Others believed that slaves should be liberated gradually. Still other abolitionists favored resettling the slave population in a foreign land, such as Central America.

Garrison and most other abolitionists thought that President Lincoln was too "soft" on slavery. Personally, Abraham Lincoln hated slavery. But he handled the explosive political issue with caution. Early in the war, Lincoln made it clear that he had launched the conflict for one reason only. "My paramount object in this struggle is to save the Union," he insisted in a letter to editor Horace Greeley, "and is not to either save or destroy slavery."

Yet, as time passed, Lincoln saw that this policy had to change. Support for the war was slipping in the North. And in Europe, English and French politicians made no secret of their sympathy for the South's "David-and-Goliath" struggle with the North. The Union cause badly needed a boost.

"All persons held as slaves within any State . . . the people whereof shall then be in rebellion against the United States, shall be then, thenceforward, and forever free." So ran the key passage in the document Lincoln issued on September 22, 1862: the Emancipation Proclamation.

Actually the proclamation freed *no* slaves right away. It called for emancipating enslaved blacks *only* in parts of the South still controlled by the Rebels. Seeing this provision, some abolitionists scorned Lincoln's act as worthless. Some Southerners agreed. Lincoln, insisted Sarah Morgan of Louisiana, "has proved himself a fool, without injuring us." Yet many other Southerners, such as Kate Stone, were outraged by "this diabolical move."

But the die was cast. The Emancipation Proclamation took effect on January 1, 1863. William Lloyd Garrison was so moved by the event that he wrote: "Thirty years ago it was midnight with the anti-slavery cause. Now it is the bright noon of day." Celebrations lit up towns and farms across the North and parts of the South. On the Sea Islands, Charlotte Forten and Colonel Thomas Higginson took part in the festivities. Forten remembered:

> As I sat on the stand and looked around . . . I thought I had never seen a sight so beautiful. There were the black soldiers, in their blue coats and scarlet pants, and crowds of lookers-on, men, women, and children. . . . The faces of all wore a happy, eager, expectant look.
>
> The exercises commenced with a prayer from Rev. Mr. Fowler. . . . Dr. Brisbane read the President's Proclamation, which was warmly cheered. Then the beautiful flags presented by Dr. Cheever's church were presented to Col. Higginson. . . . Immediately at the conclusion, some of the colored people—of their own accord sang "My Country 'Tis of Thee."

Colonel Higginson was deeply impressed by the unscheduled concert. "I never saw anything so electric . . ." he wrote later. "It seemed the choked voice of a race at last unloosed."

Across the South, agents of the Union army read the proclamation to blacks and whites alike. Some slaves were told of their emancipation by their masters. Most were not. But gradually, word spread throughout the Confederacy. In most places in the South, freedom arrived only when the Yankees did. Mary Anderson recalled Union troops sweeping through North Carolina:

> One day I heard something that sounded like thunder. . . . Next day I heard it again, boom, boom, boom. I went and asked Missus, "Is it going to rain?"
>
> . . . In a day or two . . . Marster and Missus ordered all the slaves to come to the Great House at nine o'clock. . . . Marster said, "Men, women, and children, you are free. You are no longer my slaves. The Yankees will soon be here. . . ." In about an hour there was one of the blackest clouds coming up the avenue from the main road. It was the Yankees. . . . When they left the country, lots of slaves went with them.

The news didn't reach Texas's slaves until 1865, when General Gordon Granger arrived in Galveston to subdue a Confederate force. In that state, June 19—"Juneteenth"—became the day of jubilee.

Politically, the proclamation had its desired effect. Europe saw emancipation as a noble act and chose not to take sides in America's struggle. At home, though, opponents of the president's policies struck back. In the congressional elections of November 1862, vengeful Democrats snatched 34 seats from Lincoln's Republicans. But the House of Representatives quickly bounced back with a vote of support for the proclamation.

The face of the war was changing. Although a number of Northern whites refused to fight for the freedom of slaves, many others were willing. One Indiana colonel declared, "The army will sustain the Emancipation Proclamation and enforce it with the bayonet." Up to this point, Union forces had been battling to pull the nation back together. Now they had a second purpose. In the restored Union, slavery would have no place.

Late in the war, black men were allowed to enlist in the Union ranks.
Almost all black soldiers served in segregated units.

BACKYARD BATTLEFIELDS

Wilmer McLean was not a lucky man.

On July 18, 1861, Union and Confederate forces traded shots over McLean's farm near Manassas Junction, Virginia. Around noon, a Yankee shell whistled down his chimney and exploded in his kitchen. Three days later, the battle of Manassas (known to Northerners as Bull Run) erupted in earnest. Just over a year afterward, blue and gray armies clashed at Manassas a second time.

By now, McLean had had his fill of battles in his backyard. He moved his family to a two-story brick house in a central Virginia town called Appomattox Court House. Here, in this out-of-the-way village, McLean hoped to escape the noise and havoc of the war.

THE APPROACH OF THE ENEMY

For the Confederacy, the Civil War was one long invasion. Except for a few battles, such as those at Gettysburg and Antietam, most of the war was fought across the farmlands, towns, and homesteads of the South.

The Southern states had seceded from the Union. They had ignored President Lincoln's pledge to hold the country together at all costs. It fell to the Northern armies to march into the South and bring the Rebel states to heel.

The North had to mount an aggressive war for a lofty, but sometimes vague, ideal: preserving the Union. Southerners had a clearer and more immediate purpose. Confederate soldiers were defending their homeland and way of life from the Northern invaders. They saw their fight as a sacred duty. For the civilians left behind, maintaining the home front became as noble a struggle as the conflict on the battlefields.

A Southern family packs to leave home as Union armies draw near.

The ruins of an Atlanta mansion

Some people felt this burden fell more heavily on Southern women than on their counterparts in the North. "The northern woman was never called on to endure," one Kentucky woman wrote. "She lived far from the seat of war and carnage. The sword did not cross her threshold."

The South certainly suffered the hardships of invasion more often than the North. But Northern families experienced the flash and roar of warfare in their backyards, too. On both sides, there was always the chance that the cherished home front could suddenly explode into a battlefront.

Billy Bayly was 13 years old in 1863 when the countryside around Gettysburg began to stir with news of Rebel forces in Pennsylvania. "All sorts of rumors were flying as to the approach of the enemy," he recounted afterward. He clearly remembered the "anxiety and apprehension on the part of the elders in my family, the farm hands, and neighbors." Alerted by the sound of cannon fire a few days later, Billy and two companions climbed atop a fence to get their first glimpse of the foe:

We noticed up the road, coming over the nearest hill, great masses of troops and clouds of dust . . . gray masses with the glint of steel as the sun struck the gun barrels, filling the highway, spreading out into the fields, and still coming on and on.

As the invading troops clashed with Union soldiers, the local folk's fears increased. Another Gettysburg resident, schoolteacher Sallie Robbins Broadhead, described what happened when the Confederates drew near to the town:

All was bustle and confusion. No one can imagine in what extreme fright we were when our men began to retreat. A citizen galloped up to the door in which we were sitting and called out, "For God's sake, go into the house! The Rebels are in the other end of town, and all will be killed!" We quickly ran in . . . and in a few minutes the town was full of the filthy Rebels.

Upon taking a town, invading armies occupied local homes and buildings. Here, Union soldiers and officers pose on the steps of an Atlanta house that serves as their headquarters.

Yankee troops from Massachusetts.

Some areas suffered the fear and indignity of enemy invasion more than once. Winchester, Virginia, surely held the record. The town changed hands between Yankee and Rebel forces more than 70 times in four years.

Once an invading army arrived at a town or homestead, another ugly side of war showed its face. Looting soldiers often ransacked homes and buildings in search of jewelry, silver pieces, or some kind of hidden family loot. Civilians took to burying the household silver in the ground, or hiding it in babies' cradles, invalids' beds, bird's nests, or swamps. A Richmond woman bundled kitchen utensils in a pair of her husband's long underwear and hung them from her waist. Her hoopskirt hid the loot from Yankee view, she recalled, "but as I walked and when I sat down, the clanking destroyed all hope of concealment."

Fearing looters, Helen Clifford of South Carolina fled her Charleston home with her family only to find new terror in a lonely farmhouse:

> We sprang to the door and saw an armed band . . . clad in the uniform of the Federal [Union] army, riding rapidly toward the house. . . .
>
> In a second of time the room swarmed with armed men intent on finding "the treasure." Fearful oaths and threats were heard as they explored the house from cellar to garret. . . . Haversacks and pockets were filled, and when no dent of pressing could put more into them, snowy cases were drawn from pillows and converted into sacks into which they stored their booty.

Helen's brother Earle was seized by the soldiers and questioned about hidden gold. When Earle didn't—or couldn't—give the soldiers information, he was bound and strung up to a tree. Only the timely arrival of sympathetic Union officers saved the day and—literally—Earle's neck.

Women were not spared the brutalities of an invasion. White and black women were sometimes raped by invading soldiers. Other civilians did not even escape with their lives. Of those who didn't, 20-year-old Mary Virginia Wade of Gettysburg is perhaps the best known. Rising early on the third day of the battle there, "Ginny" was in the kitchen making breakfast for her sick sister. A bullet from a Rebel sharpshooter ripped through two doors before striking Ginny in the head. The Gettysburg *Star and Banner* called her death "the saddest event connected with the battle."

"A QUIET STATE OF TERROR"

The wave of plunder by invading armies was not always unstoppable. Defiant home owners and their families and slaves sometimes thwarted looters by sheer pluck and ingenuity. Hearing of the approach of the Confederates in 1862, a farmer in Sharpsburg, Maryland, acted swiftly to protect his livestock. He herded his horses into the dank darkness of his cellar. Then he fastened feedbags to their hooves to muffle the noise of their movements. The unsuspecting Rebels who crisscrossed the farmer's property never heard a thing.

Other civilians "killed" enemy invaders with kindness. Union General Franz Sigel and his troops bivouacked outside a wealthy woman's mansion in Rappahannock County, Virginia. One afternoon, the general and his staff paid the woman a call. Calmly and with dignity, she rang for her servant. "John," she instructed him, "tea for fourteen, please." For the rest of the afternoon, she charmed her "guests" by singing "Dixie," "The Bonnie Blue Flag," and other Southern favorites. Accompanying her at the piano was General Sigel himself. No damage was done to the woman's property.

But the carnage went on. The enemy did not even have to be near to be deadly. Often, the invading force conducted its attack by siege— surrounding an enemy city and pounding it from a safe distance with

During the 47-day siege of Vicksburg, Union soldiers lived in these hillside dugouts near the city.

artillery fire. Such a tactic was used by Union forces against Vicksburg, Mississippi, in the summer of 1863. Like many other residents, Mary Ann Loughborough tried to escape the shelling by taking refuge in a cave dug out of nearby bluffs. She never forgot the nightmare of the relentless bombardment:

> My heart stood still as we would hear the report from the guns, and the rushing and fearful sound of the shell as it came toward us. As it neared, the noise became more deafening; the air was full of the rushing sound; pains darted through my temples; my ears were full of the confusing noise; and as it exploded, the report flashed through my head like an electric shock, leaving me in a quiet state of terror.

In some cases, enemy shelling became so intense that residents were forced to leave their hometowns entirely and quickly. In 1862 Annie Coulson Harper and her parents were caught by surprise when a Federal gunboat began lobbing shells at their Mississippi town. "Thicker and faster they came, and soon Natchez was the scene of a panic terrible to behold," she later recorded. Annie and her family witnessed the fear and confusion as residents poured into the streets:

> The roads leading from the town were filled with a stampeding throng. On foot were bareheaded women with a child under each arm fleeing from the wrath behind them. Horses, carts, drays, dogs, mules, wheelbarrows, carriages, and people in an indiscriminate melee rushing as they supposed from the City of Destruction. . . . One little girl running up the hill leading from the landing was killed by a piece of shell. Two other persons were wounded.

THE AFTERMATH OF BATTLE

When the attack or siege had ended, the troubles for the people left behind did not disappear. Northerners and Southerners shared one common result after a battle: casualties. Makeshift hospitals were quickly set up to treat the wounded, and local citizens often pitched in. Sallie Robbins Broadhead helped tend Federal soldiers in the local seminary after heavy rains soaked the battlefield at Gettysburg. To her shock, she discovered that more than wounds and infections threatened the patients:

> Worse horrors met my eyes on descending to the basement of the building. Men, wounded in three and four places, not able to help themselves the least bit, lay almost swimming in water. I hunted the lady whom I had been helping. . . . When she came down she reverently exclaimed, "My God! they must be gotten out of this or they will drown. . . ."
>
> By hard work she had it accomplished. We had the satisfaction of seeing them comfortably fixed . . . dry and thankful for so little.

The home front-turned-battlefield-turned-hospital zone had still another problem to contend with. Not only did war exact a fearful price in

Another aftereffect of battle: hundreds—sometimes thousands—of dead bodies. These men died at Antietam, Maryland.

Richmond in ruins, 1865

human life, but it also took its toll on homes and property. What could not be smashed, broken, or carried away might be trampled, twisted, or put to the torch.

Easily the worst mass destruction of the Civil War took place during the infamous march across the South of Union General William Tecumseh Sherman. In late 1864 and early 1865, Sherman and 62,000 troops marched from Atlanta to Savannah, Georgia, to Columbia, South Carolina, and to central North Carolina. Behind them they left a smoldering trail of leveled warehouses, demolished bridges, burned houses, and twisted train rails. "Bummers" (looters) made off with horses, mules, cattle, and hogs to feed Sherman's marauding army. Great cities such as Atlanta and Columbia were left in ashes.

"The entire heart of the city is a wilderness of crumbling walls, naked chimneys, and trees killed by the flames," a Northern journalist wrote of

General Sherman was determined to crush the South on his famous "March to the Sea."

Columbia. "The fountains of the desolated gardens are dry, the basins cracked; the pillars of the houses are dismantled. . . . All these attest to the wealth and elegance which one night of fire and orgy sufficed to destroy."

Sherman's strategy was simple. He aimed to crush the spirit of the South's civilians to help defeat its army. "We cannot change the hearts of these people of the South," he said, "but we can make war so terrible . . . that generations will pass away before they again appeal to it." He was as good as his word. By war's end, Sherman's hordes had done $100 million in damage across a vast swath of the South more than 400 miles long.

Anna Maria Green of Milledgeville, Georgia—then the state capital—witnessed the departure of Sherman's troops from her home. For her as for thousands of others on the Southern home front, the destruction had two effects. One, of course, was physical; the other was deeply emotional. "This morning the last of the vandals left our city and burned the bridge after them—leaving suffering and desolation behind them, and embittering every heart."

The war was not through with Wilmer McLean. April 1865 found the legions of Robert E. Lee and Ulysses S. Grant arrayed across the countryside near Appomattox Court House. Outnumbered, hungry, and fought to a standstill, General Lee's Army of Northern Virginia could do no more. Lee arranged to meet Lieutenant General Grant to discuss terms of surrender. A Union officer approached McLean to find a suitable place for the meeting. Reluctantly, he agreed to the use of his own home. There, in McLean's living room, the two great generals signed the papers that ended the Civil War.

According to legend, Wilmer McLean had the last word. "The war began in my front yard," he declared, "and it ended in my front parlor."

Wilmer McLean's home in Appomattox Court House, Virginia—the site of Robert E. Lee's surrender

SHOULDERING THE LOAD

As thousands of young men hurried to enlist in their home-state regiments, millions more Americans prepared for their own struggles on the home front. The war effort drained resources on both sides. Already at a disadvantage, the South suffered the most serious shortages. A Union naval blockade closed off Southern ports, one by one. Everyday household items such as needles, pins, soap, matches, candles, kettles, linens, oil, and coal grew more rare as the war dragged on.

In Mississippi, Annie Coulson Harper lamented the shrinking supply of foodstuffs. "Flour became scarce," she recalled. "Coffee was hoarded as gold dust and sugar was very high. . . . Fortunately, the hens did not refuse to lay or the cows to give milk, or sad would have been our lot." The fledgling armies required vast amounts of food, shoes, medicines, and cloth for uniforms. Whatever resources were available went to troops first, civilians last. When morphine, chloroform, quinine, and other drugs ran out on the home front, residents turned to nature for substitutes. "The woods . . . were . . . our drug store," one Southerner said. Citizens scoured forests and fields for dandelions, snakeroot, skunk cabbage, and pokeweed, as well as turpentine and other natural "remedies."

Businesses were also hit hard. When paper ran low, newspaper publishers resorted to printing some editions on the back of wallpaper. Books and school supplies were hard to come by. One of the few Southern arithmetic primers published during the war offered this problem: "If one Confederate soldier can whip 7 Yankees, how many soldiers can whip 49 Yankees?"

As supplies ran low, prices skyrocketed. A popular joke said that shoppers took their money to market in bushel baskets and brought home purchases in their pocketbooks. A pound of butter sold for $3.50 in Southern markets in early 1863. In a year, the price rose 700 percent, to $25.00 per pound.

Wages lagged pitifully behind the soaring costs. J. B. Jones worked as a Confederate clerk in Richmond, Virginia, making $3,000 a year. He noted these prices in August 1863: flour at $40 a barrel, coal at $25 per cartload, and wood, $30 per cord. On January 9, 1865, Jones made a rueful entry in his diary: "Flour is $700 a barrel to-day; meal $80 per bushel; coal and wood, $100 per load. Does the government . . . mean to allow the rich speculators, the quartermasters, etc., to starve honest men into the Union?"

Consumers in the North did not suffer such severe shortages as those in the South. But as goods became more scarce, costs went higher. Between 1861 and 1863, prices in the Union states increased by one-half, while wages rose by only one-tenth.

The continuing call for more soldiers robbed stores of clerks, banks of tellers, and medical offices of doctors. In time, even craftsmen and iron-workers—men whose skills were vital to the defense industry—were drafted. Schools also suffered. "I have the military fever very strong," a teacher in North Carolina explained to his superintendent. As young and middle-aged men left home to join up, women sometimes stepped in to serve as instructors. But very often, schools had no choice but to close. "Students have all gone to war," the faculty secretary of one Southern college reported in 1861. "College suspended, and God help the right."

"OUR FINGERS WERE NEVER IDLE"

Most of the adults left behind the battle were young and middle-aged women. On this group fell a double burden. One was to keep homesteads and farms running without the help of their husbands, sons, and brothers. The second burden was to support the soldiers at the battlefront. Judith McGuire knew the weight of this responsibility. "While men are making a free-will offering of their life's blood on the altar of their country," she wrote, "women must not be idle."

Across the land, women shouldered the load left by the absent men. In cities, they took jobs in government and industry. They toiled for low pay, often in poor conditions. In rural areas, the scene was similar. Social worker Mary Livermore traveled the wheat lands of Wisconsin and Iowa in 1863 and recorded what she saw: "Women were in the field everywhere, driving the reapers, binding and shocking, and loading grain, until then an unusual sight." A well-known song of the period echoed that theme:

> Just take your gun and go,
> for Ruth can drive the oxen, John,
> and I can use the hoe.

In the war's early months, even the wealthier, better-equipped North had to rush to catch up with the needs of its new armies. Huge numbers of recruits on both sides overwhelmed their governments. Uniforms and supplies could not be produced quickly enough. Civilians tried to take up the slack.

North and South, women and girls met in homes, schools, and churches to form sewing circles. Their output was remarkable. One band in Boston turned out a thousand shirts in one day. "Our fingers were never idle," Rose Frye of Kentucky remembered. "I have seen the most

The Soldier's Aid Society of Springfield, Illinois, has readied food and clothing for Union troops.

delicate fingers toiling over a coarse fly tent, coarse jean trousers or jacket, heavy woolen shirt, cloth cap, and cloth overcoat. We quilted comforts. We pieced quilts. We made carpets. We utilized every stray rag or paper which came our way." Mounting casualties meant a rising need for bandages. Literally tons of lint were scraped from old linen cloth to make medical dressings. To keep pace with the demand, even the youngest girls and boys helped perform this chore.

In the North, groups of young women calling themselves Alert Clubs canvassed their towns asking neighbors for used clothing. To collect the

Executive Mansion
Washington, Nov 21. 1864

To Mrs Bixby, Boston, Mass,

Dear Madam.

I have been shown in the files
of the War Department a statement of the Adjutant
General of Massachusetts that you are the mother of
five sons who have died gloriously on the field of battle
I feel how weak and fruitless must be any word of
mine which should attempt to beguile you from the
grief of a loss so overwhelming. But I cannot refrain
from tendering you the consolation that may be found
in the thanks of the republic they died to save I
pray that our Heavenly Father may assuage the anguish
of your bereavement, and leave you only the cherished
memory of the loved and lost, and the solemn pride
that must be yours to have laid so costly a sacrifice
upon the altar of freedom

Yours very sincerely and respectfully.

A. Lincoln.

One Boston mother lost five sons in battle. Her small consolation: a letter from President Lincoln himself.

donations, groups of boys dubbed "Minute Men" hauled wheelbarrows and wagons. Boys and girls in New Haven, Connecticut, organized a Fourth of July Fruit Fund to raise money to buy fruit for soldiers in the field.

THE PRICE OF DUTY

The most difficult task on the home front lay in keeping hope alive as loved ones risked death in battle. Separation, distance, and uncertainty were the triple torments suffered by those left at home. Casualty lists appeared periodically in newspapers, bringing the news families dreaded most. "The daily 'Extras' could not be printed fast enough to satisfy the anxious impatient hearts," Annie Harper recorded. "When the news came of a battle in which our boys were engaged, wives and mothers would flock to the telegraph office and wait for dispatches with a consuming anxiety that was pitiful to look at."

For those who had more than one relative in uniform, the fear was multiplied. One Southern woman who had five sons in the army described her dilemma: "I lie awake night after night, count each stroke of the clock, dread both night and day, tremble to open a letter."

When the worst news came, it struck swift and deep. Early in 1864, Sarah Morgan of Baton Rouge received a double shock: two of her brothers fighting in the Rebel army had died of disease. Grief-stricken, Morgan poured her anguish into her diary. "O my brothers! What have we lived for except you? We who would so gladly have laid down our lives for yours, are left desolate to mourn over all we loved and hoped for . . . God help us!"

Not every young man was eager to make such a sacrifice. The wild enthusiasm for war following Fort Sumter began to fade soon after the casualties began arriving home. In April 1862, the South enacted the nation's first military draft. Able-bodied men between the ages of 18 and 35 were tapped for service in the Confederate army. But any man who owned 20 or more slaves was exempt (excused) from service. In the North, the law allowed men to avoid military service for a price. For a $300 fee, a man could purchase an exemption. North and South, a

Advertisements encouraged men to sign up as substitute soldiers—and to receive a generous payment—before they got drafted.

draftee could hire a substitute to fight in his place for anywhere from $200 to $1,000—sometimes more.

Many people found this practice unfair and unpatriotic. An 1862 cartoon shows a well-dressed young man, hat in hand, greeting his sweetheart with the exclamation, "Ah! Dearest Addie! I've succeeded. I've got a substitute!"

"Have you?" the young lady replies. "What a curious coincidence! And *I* have found one for YOU!"

THE BUSINESS OF WAR

Two days after the first battle of Manassas, the fields and woods were quiet. No rifles cracked, no cannon thundered, no men shouted and cursed. But behind the stillness, another type of action was taking place. The scene of the war's first clash and the North's first defeat was the object of tremendous public interest. Realizing this fact, real estate dealers purchased much of the battlefield. Their purpose: to charge curious visitors an admission fee to see the now-famous landmark.

While many on the home front suffered and sacrificed during the war, other enterprising men and women turned a profit on it. Some did so honestly. Others did not mind taking advantage of their government to do it.

Two Northern businessmen had profiteering down to a science. Arthur Eastman purchased a large number of used rifles from the U.S. War Department for $3.50 each. These he sold for $12.50 apiece to a second speculator named Simon Stevens. Not to be outdone in profit-making, Stevens sold the same rifles back to the Union army for $22.00 apiece.

The stock market provided another gold mine for shady dealers. In the 1860s, future millionaire Jay Gould began building his personal fortune on the fortunes of war. Knowing that stock prices rose and fell with the Union army's wins and defeats, Gould tapped an inside source. A government agent secretly fed him news of the latest Federal loss or victory before the public was informed. Gould used this information to get the jump on market reaction, and he bought and sold his way to wealth.

Southerners devised their own schemes. For decades, English textile manufacturers had depended on the South for cotton. Once the war began, the Confederate government stopped selling cotton to England, refusing to ship more until England gave its support to the Confederacy. Rebel leaders hoped that desperate English factory owners would press their government to support the Confederacy and restore their cotton supply. Instead, England began looking for new sources of cotton, and some Southern planters did the unthinkable. Hiding large shipments from the eyes of Confederate authorities, they secretly sold the cotton to agents of their enemy, the North.

Although most Northern manufacturers couldn't purchase cotton during the war, they suffered little from the loss. Many Yankee clothing-makers switched to wool. Others simply switched businesses. Connecticut cotton-goods manufacturer James Mowry did not panic when the cotton shortage hit. Quickly shifting gears, Mowry converted his textile mill into a weapons assembly plant. Then he landed a handsome government contract to produce 30,000 rifles for the U.S. Army. A year later, his factory was turning out 1,200 rifles per week.

Factories needed fuel, and Northern industrialists rushed to provide it. The first fields to yield petroleum were on Oil Creek in western

New industries emerged during the war. Based in Pennsylvania, the petroleum business boomed.

Pennsylvania. By the end of 1861, the wells there were giving up as much as 2,500 barrels a day. Shrewd investors like Andrew Carnegie and John D. Rockefeller entered the oil business during the war and grew wealthy from their dealings in the "black gold." As a sign in New York proclaimed in 1865: "Oil is Now King, Not Cotton."

Industry thrived on wartime needs, and civilians benefited too. Elias Howe's sewing machine, patented in the 1840s, had already sped up clothing production. But when the war began, shirts, trousers, and dresses were still produced mostly in tailor shops for the rich and at home for the not-so-rich. Now armies had to clothe thousands of men in uniforms that needed to fit reasonably well. The government solved that problem by ordering uniforms from suppliers in a set of standard sizes. Any one size was bound to fit a large segment of the military population. Soldiers now had better fitting uniforms, and the ready-made, standardized clothing industry had arrived to stay.

Smaller businessmen—portrait photographers, saloon-keepers, and barbers—did a brisk business when armies of men arrived in town. Prostitutes were also quick to cash in on the needs of men in uniform. Groups of "working girls" followed both Northern and Southern armies to camp. Union General Joseph Hooker was said to be unusually permissive about his men's leisure time. Legend has it that prostitutes who frequented the general's camps first earned the now-famous nickname, "hookers."

Caissons loaded with ammunition at a Federal supply depot in Virginia. Manufacturers who provided equipment, food, and uniforms to the army often grew rich.

WARFARE IN THE WARDS

Bearing the bandages, water, and
  sponge,
Straight and swift to my wounded
  I go,
Where they lie on the ground,
After the battle brought in.
                    —Walt Whitman,
        "The Wound Dresser," 1865

One day in 1861, New York lawyer George Templeton Strong entered the building that housed his law offices. The first floor had been converted into temporary quarters for Federal soldiers traveling through the city. Strong's nose instantly alerted him to the presence of the troops. "I never knew before what rankness of stench can be emitted by unwashed humanity," he wrote in his diary. "It half strangles me as I go upstairs." With this pungent introduction to the problem of poor sanitation in the army, Strong went to work. Joined by other prominent citizens, he helped to found the United States Sanitary Commission.

The unsanitary conditions that marked Civil War camps and hospitals were not only unpleasant but also dangerous. Garbage, rotting scraps of food, and human and animal waste fouled the grounds and bred disease. Typhoid, dysentery, scurvy, pneumonia, and diphtheria were rampant.

The new Sanitary Commission had its work cut out for it. Frederick Law Olmsted, a New York landscape architect, was selected to head its efforts. His first task was to draw together 7,000 local soldiers' aid societies scattered across the North. By coordinating shipping locations and schedules, he organized the transport of food, medicine, and other supplies to far-flung battle sites. Meanwhile, a battalion of sanitary inspectors traveled to camps and hospitals. These roving commissioners insisted on cleaner conditions, properly prepared food, and the fair distribution of mail, medicine, and clothing.

Much of the commission's work was performed by women. Chicagoan Mary Livermore organized 3,000 local aid chapters across the Midwest. Her Chicago branch alone shipped 30,000 boxes of supplies in its first two years. Dr. Elizabeth Blackwell, the first licensed female physician in the United States, assembled thousands of volunteers into the Women's Central Association of Relief. At first denied official recognition, the WCAR was soon made a major branch of the Sanitary Commission.

Not all Union hospitals were this orderly and spacious. Often, wounded soldiers were placed in makeshift wards: the halls of public buildings, church basements, private homes, tents, or just outdoors in clearings.

As wagonloads of supplies rolled out, money ran low. In their search for badly needed funds, Chicago volunteers hit on a novel idea. Issuing appeals for donations, the commission planned a wartime extravaganza, complete with parades, refreshments, and exhibits. From several states came offerings of pianos, sewing machines, silverware, clothing, fruit, and livestock. These were displayed in six flag-draped exposition halls. The nation's first sanitary fair opened in the fall of 1863 and was expected to raise $25,000 for soldiers' aid. Instead, the two-week event brought in $100,000. Soon, similar fairs sprang up in New York, Boston, Philadelphia, and other cities.

The South could not imitate the spectacular success of the Northern fairs. Lacking the wealth and transportation systems of the North, the Confederacy had no sanitary commission. "With us," a Southerner wrote, "every house was a hospital."

MEDICINE AND MERCY

At the end of 1862, a 43-year-old poet from Brooklyn scoured a Virginia field hospital in search of his wounded brother. To Walt Whitman, the scenes of suffering in the wards were appalling. He was so moved by what he saw that he traveled to Washington, D.C., to be near the casualties that filled its hospitals. Following the battle of Chancellorsville, he described the wounded in their camps:

> There they lie . . . in an open space in the woods, from 200 to 300 poor fellows—the groans and screams—the odor of blood mixing with the scent of the night . . . one man is shot by a shell, both in the arm and leg—both are amputated. . . . Some have their legs blown off—some, bullets through the breast—some, indescribably horrid wounds in the face or head.

Whitman spent the rest of the war haunting the hospital wards. Here, he dispensed what comfort he could, giving out spending money and sweets, writing letters, changing dressings, and sharing conversation. He would later write of his Civil War experiences in poetry and prose collected in such works as *Drum Taps* and *Specimen Days*.

Dealing with the frightening torrent of sick and wounded pouring in from the battlefields was a staggering challenge. North and South, hospitals of all sizes sprang up everywhere. The largest was Chimborazo Hospital in Richmond, Virginia, with 8,000 beds. Churches, hotels, schoolhouses, barns, and private homes were all put to use as hospitals. The Virginia mansion of Confederate general Robert E. Lee sheltered hundreds of Union casualties. In Washington, D.C., stricken Yankees were housed in the Rotunda and Congress of the Capitol building. Even the nearby Georgetown prison was cleared to make room for incoming wounded.

The most successful hospital was operated by Sally Tompkins of Richmond. Borrowing the house of a local judge and paying all the expenses, Tompkins directed six nurses in tending 1,333 patients over four years. Of those patients, only 73 died. It was the best survival record on either side of the war.

The quality of Civil War medical care was uneven at best. So was the training of surgeons. Many doctors had learned their skills as apprentices, with hands-on training but little or no classroom instruction.

"Every house was a hospital." A Southern woman makes "hoe-cake for a sick Rebel" explains the caption of this wartime lithograph.

Newer doctors often held a diploma of some sort from a medical school. But a surprising number of both types had never used thermometers, stethoscopes, or syringes, even though these instruments were common in Europe. About 13,000 physicians served the Union cause in the field and in regular hospitals. Less than one-third of that number served the South.

Battlefield surgery was a medieval nightmare. Artillery and minié balls—roundheaded bullets—did terrible damage to men's bodies. Shattered arms and legs were often treated in the same fashion: by amputation. Crude bone saws, knives, and tourniquets were the chief tools used to get the grisly job done. One Union general recalled the scene in a field hospital after the Battle of the Wilderness: "A wounded man was lifted on the table, often shrieking with pain. . . . The surgeon snatched his knife from between his teeth . . . wiped it rapidly once or twice across

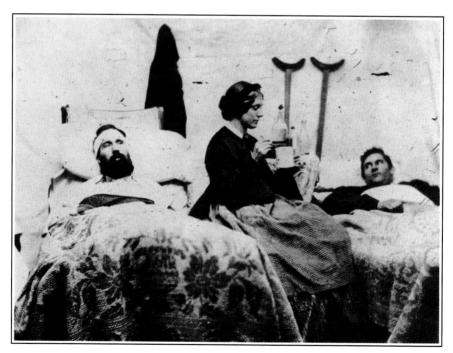

Nurse Anne Bell with patients at a Nashville hospital. More men died from infection and disease than from battle wounds during the Civil War.

his blood-stained apron, and the cutting began." On the Federal side, an estimated three out of every four operations were amputations. About one-fourth of those patients died.

For anesthesia, ether and chloroform were used. Opium and morphine deadened pain before and after surgery. The most common dressing for wounds was lint, usually applied wet and later moistened with water to prevent its drying out. Broken limbs were set with wood splints or plaster of paris.

"BETWEEN BULLET AND BATTLEFIELD"

As horrible as battlefield wounds could be, an even greater killer stalked Civil War hospital wards. Disease claimed the lives of two men for every one man killed in combat. Like Walt Whitman, author Louisa May Alcott tended wounded soldiers in Union hospitals. At one point she was assigned to a 40-bed ward, "where I spent my shining hours washing faces, serving rations, giving medicines, and sitting in a very hard chair with pneumonia on one side, diphtheria on the other, five typhoids on the opposite."

A variety of drugs were employed to combat the fearful array of illnesses and infections. Quinine was the universal drug of the war. It was liberally doled out to patients suffering from malaria, rheumatism, neuralgia, syphilis, diarrhea, and fevers. The deadly invasion of gangrene—a rotting of the flesh caused by poor blood flow or bacteria—was battled with nitric acid, chlorine, bromine, and surgery.

The Civil War saw an important addition to American medicine: women. Before the 1850s, only men worked as nurses and hospital attendants. But led by the pioneering English nurse Florence Nightingale, women entered nursing during the Crimean War (1853–1856). Throughout the Civil War, some 3,000 women served the ill and wounded on the Northern side alone. The most famous of these was Clara Barton.

When a Baltimore mob attacked a regiment from her home state of Massachusetts, Barton, then working in Washington, D.C., went into action. She gathered provisions and delivered them to the wounded

Clara Barton

Dorothea Dix

being sheltered in the Capitol. Then she expanded her operations by hauling wagonloads of supplies to army camps and battle zones. Barton believed her place was "anywhere between the bullet and the battlefield." Sometimes it was closer than that. At Antietam, Maryland, a stray Rebel bullet tore through her sleeve and killed the patient she was treating. After the war, she went on to greater fame by founding the American chapter of the Red Cross.

Mary Ann Bickerdyke, a Sanitary Commission agent, set up Union hospitals and tirelessly nursed soldiers at 19 different battles. Although her manner was brittle, her efforts were successful. When a surgeon complained about her to General Sherman, he was told, "If it was Bickerdyke, I can't do anything for you. She ranks me."

Dorothea Dix, a champion for better treatment of the mentally ill, pursued a plan for a female nursing corps with relentless devotion. When her idea was rejected by Washington politicians, she formed the corps anyway. Later she was officially named its superintendent. Dix's requirements for her nurses were strict, as young Cornelia Hancock soon learned. Hancock journeyed to Baltimore, hoping to help care for the hordes of wounded coming in from Gettysburg:

> Here Dorothea Dix appeared on the scene. She looked the nurses over and pronounced them all suitable except me. She immediately objected to my going further on the score of my youth and rosy cheeks . . . I was then just twenty-three. Such a thing as a hospital corps of comely young maiden nurses, possessing grace and looks, was then unknown.

Hancock at last succeeded in reaching Gettysburg and plunged into her work. Like most of her colleagues, she soon grew used to the gruesome realities of tending torn and shattered bodies. "I do not mind the sight of blood," she wrote in a letter home, "have seen limbs taken off and was not sick at all." But the gentler side of caring for her patients was sometimes more troubling. "I would get on first rate if they would not ask me to write to [their] wives," she added. "*That* I cannot do without crying."

Even hardened veterans of the wards could be overcome by the tragedy and waste of the war. Phoebe Yates Pember, matron of Chimborazo Hospital, recorded an incident in which a young patient's leg had been badly splintered in battle. One evening a bone fragment ruptured one of his arteries. Pember placed her finger over the wound to stop the small gusher of blood. When informed by the surgeon that nothing could be done, the patient asked, "How long can I live?"

"Only as long as I keep my finger on this artery," Pember replied. The young man pondered for a moment. "You can let go," he said at last. "Hot tears rushed to my eyes, a surging sound to my ears, and a deathly coldness to my lips," Pember related. "The pang of obeying him was spared me . . . I fainted away."

VOICES OF HOME

I have seen Him in the watch-fires
of a hundred circling camps;
They have builded Him an altar
in the evening dews and damps;
I can read His righteous sentence
by the dim and flaring lamps.
His day is marching on.

—Julia Ward Howe,
"Battle Hymn of the Republic,"
1861

The staccato crack-crack of rifle shots shattered the calm of the late-autumn Virginia morning. Across the Rappahannock River, Confederate sharpshooters perched in church steeples in the town of Fredericksburg. From there they poured a killing fire down on Union engineers intent on building a pontoon bridge to span the river.

While bullets whined and men dropped, a solitary figure went calmly about his business. Timothy O'Sullivan quietly loaded an eight-by-ten-inch glass plate into a large boxlike object on thin wooden legs. After 30 seconds or so, he removed the plate and rushed it to a nearby horse-drawn wagon. Inside its tentlike interior, O'Sullivan slid the plate into a tray of chemicals. Had they had time to notice, the embattled engineers might have seen what few people in America had ever beheld. Timothy O'Sullivan was taking photographs.

Photography was less than a quarter-century old when the Civil War began. Up to that time, almost all photographs were made in city studios with bulky portrait cameras. But when war began, photographers moved to the battlefields. Battle locations shifted regularly, so photographers had to be ready to move quickly—and often. While journalists and sketch artists had only their pencils and papers to tote, combat cameramen had entire darkrooms to carry with them. Tents mounted on horse-drawn wagons served as both darkrooms and storage areas.

The most popular method of field photography was the so-called wet process. A glass plate was coated with a syrupy liquid called collodion and bathed in a silver nitrate solution. Because exposure times were long—it took up to half a minute to snap a picture—it was nearly impossible for photographers to capture the fast-moving action of battle. Even slower moving dogs, cats, and people on foot often appear as transparent "ghosts" in early photographs.

For a small fee, soldiers could have a picture made at a traveling photography studio.

Among the first Civil War photographers—and easily the best-known—was Mathew Brady. Already famous for his studio pictures, Brady was fascinated by the possibilities of using a camera to capture the sights of war for history. In 1861 he visited Union camps and the battle site at Bull Run. "A spirit in my feet said 'go,'" he wrote later, "and I went."

Many if not all of Brady's battlefield pictures were actually taken by assistants like Timothy O'Sullivan, James Gibson, and T. C. Roche. Another Brady assistant, gallery manager Alexander Gardner, created some of the best portraits of Abraham Lincoln before the president's assassination in 1865.

Despite cumbersome equipment and clumsy techniques, Civil War cameramen produced remarkable pictures. Life in army camps, cannon crews at work, caravans crossing rivers, and wounded soldiers in hospitals were all captured by the sluggish eye of the camera. For civilians on the home front, these images of war had a startling effect. After viewing Mathew Brady's photo exhibit titled *The Dead of Antietam*, a *New York Times* reporter was deeply moved. "If [Brady] has not brought bodies and laid them in our door yards and along our streets," he wrote, "he has done something very like it."

Photography had a more personal meaning for the soldiers themselves. In the field, both raw recruits and seasoned officers lined up outside traveling studios to have their portraits made. These they mailed back home to parents, brothers and sisters, and sweethearts. For some families, such a photograph was their last look at a loved one lost in battle.

PENCIL AND SKETCHBOOK

If the shutter of the camera could not freeze the frenzied pace of war action, sharp eyes and swift hands could. A small regiment of special artists traveled the same dusty roads and swollen rivers as the battle-worn armies. Dispatched by weekly illustrated newspapers to cover the war, "specials" did so at their own risk. The work was hazardous and the pay was low. Bullets, enemy shells, capture, and disease were perils shared by the artists and soldiers alike.

Suspicion and hostility were other problems that specials encountered. Grumbling over "reporters," Federal general William T. Sherman once ejected artist Henri Lovie from his camp. Lovie protested that he was "no reporter or correspondent, not writing more than a brief description of my sketches."

Sherman was not persuaded. "You fellows make the best-paid spies that can be bought," he retorted. "Jeff Davis owes more to you newspaper men than to his army."

Two of the best of the special artists were the English-born brothers Alfred and William Waud. William, along with Edwin Forbes, German-born Thomas Nast, and others, turned out dozens of pencil sketches and wash drawings for *Frank Leslie's Illustrated Newspaper*. Alfred began his wartime career sketching for the *New York Illustrated News*. Fierce competition for artistic talent among rival papers, however, landed both brothers on the payroll of *Harper's Weekly* by 1863.

Artists like Alfred Waud, pictured here at Gettysburg, Pennsylvania, risked their lives to record the sights of battle.

The Army of the Potomac attempts to cross the Rappahannock River, January 20, 1863. This illustration by Alfred Waud appeared in **Harper's Weekly.**

These publications did not feature photographs, since no process had yet been invented for reproducing photos in print. Hand-drawn art had no such limitations. To make the leap from sketch pad to printed page, an illustration had only to be specially prepared. The sketch was given to an engraver, who traced and engraved the drawing onto a block of box-wood. This time-consuming procedure took three to four weeks. Then someone (possibly Frank Leslie himself) came up with the idea of having four engravers work on the same picture at once—each reproducing one-quarter of the image. This process brought images of battle to news-starved readers in half the time as before.

THE SPIRIT OF MUSIC

Once, after attending a band concert, Robert E. Lee remarked, "I don't think we can have an army without music." Indeed, the emotions roused by the struggle of the Civil War found an ideal outlet in a blossoming art form: the popular song.

In melody and lyric, songwriters expressed the pride, affection, determination, and hope of both regions. The great Southern ballad "Lorena" tells of a man's tribute to life and love:

> The sun's low down the sky, Lorena,
> The frost gleams where the flowers have been.
> But the heart throbs on as warmly now
> As when summer days were nigh.

Confederate loyalty and love of the land are exalted in "The Bonnie Blue Flag":

> We are a band of brothers, and native to the soil,
> Fighting for the property we gained by honest toil.

Ironically, the most renowned Confederate song was not composed by a Southerner. The classic "Dixie" was actually written by a Northerner for a New York minstrel show.

The North had its share of wartime favorites too. The most enduring of these songs was penned in 1861. After witnessing a Union troop review in Washington, D.C., Julia Ward Howe went back to her hotel and to bed. In her ears lingered the strains of the song "John Brown's Body." Inspiration was soon to follow:

> I awoke in the gray of the morning twilight, and . . . the long gray lines of the desired poem began to twine themselves in my mind . . . I sprang out of bed and . . . scrawled the verses almost without looking at the paper.

The poem was published in the *Atlantic Monthly* under the title, "The Battle-hymn of the Republic." Once it was set to the "John Brown's Body" melody, it became an instant hit.

In 1861, 22-year-old James Randall Ryder composed a poem urging his home state of Maryland to leave the Union. Titled "Maryland, My Maryland" and sung to the tune of "O Tannenbaum," the song failed to

Harriet Beecher Stowe's novel Uncle Tom's Cabin *fired up anti-slavery feelings in the North. On meeting Stowe, President Lincoln reportedly said, "So you're the little woman that made this great war."*

Walt Whitman became caught up in the conflict when his brother George was wounded in battle in late 1862.

lure the state into the Confederacy. The next year, Robert E. Lee's Rebel troops invaded the state. They were ordered to sing Ryder's song in hopes of turning the residents against the North. Once again, the song changed nobody's mind.

THE POWER OF WORDS

The North was thrilled and outraged. The South was indignant and angry. In England, Queen Victoria and the wife of author Charles Dickens cried. The cause of this outpouring of feeling was a book. The year was 1852, and Harriet Beecher Stowe had just published her novel of slavery in the Old South, *Uncle Tom's Cabin*. It caused a sensation. Readers at home and abroad were swept up in Stowe's tragic tale of the noble old slave Tom, the child Topsy, and the evil New England overseer Simon Legree. The dramatic scene in which the young slave Eliza flees from Legree and his hounds over a frozen river caught the public's imagination and sympathy. Although Southerners claimed the book painted a lopsided picture of slavery, aroused Northerners joined the abolitionist ranks in droves. The book was the Civil War's greatest propaganda work.

Poets added rhythm and meter to the torrent of words that gave voice to wartime emotions. Bret Harte, Oliver Wendell Holmes, Herman Melville, Henry Timrod, and others created a large body of poetry for eager readers. Some Civil War verse was lofty and sentimental. Yet much of it dealt directly with everyday tragedies and triumphs. In "Come Up From the Fields, Father," Walt Whitman explored the anguish of home-front families who had sons in battle:

> Come up from the fields, father, here's a letter from our Pete,
> And come to the front door, mother, here's a letter from thy
>   dear son.

The letter tells the family only that Pete has been wounded in a skirmish. They have no way yet of knowing the cruel truth:

> Alas, poor boy, he will never be better...
> While they stand at home at the door he is dead already,
> The only son is dead.

Other poets gushed in undisguised admiration for the war's heroes. Kate Brownlee Sherwood penned the praises of a Confederate general in "Albert Sidney Johnston":

> But ever while we sing of war, of courage tried and true,
> Of heroes wed to gallant deeds, or be it Gray or Blue,
> Then Albert Sidney Johnston's name shall flash before
>   our sight
> Like some resplendent meteor across the somber night.

No matter how grim and brutal the war became, Americans still managed to laugh occasionally. Daily papers and illustrated weeklies ran columns and features with short, humorous items to lighten the news of

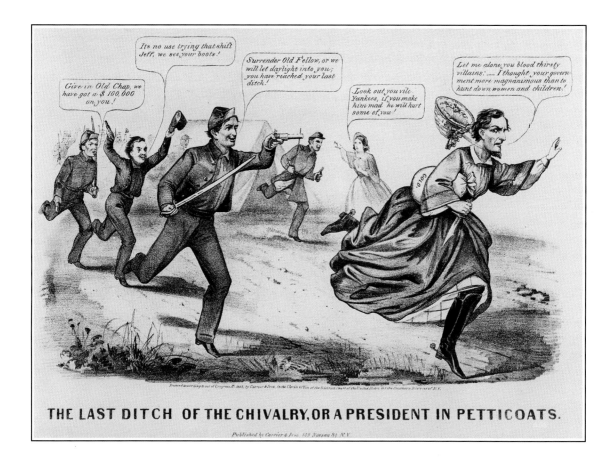

THE LAST DITCH OF THE CHIVALRY, OR A PRESIDENT IN PETTICOATS.

battles and casualties. The "Humors of the Day" column in an 1862 issue of *Harper's Weekly* amused readers with this imaginary conversation between a married couple: "Now do take this medicine, wife, and I'll be hanged if it doesn't cure you."

"Oh, I will take it then," his wife responds, "for it is sure to do good one way or the other."

Humorists such as David R. Locke and Josh Billings found a ready audience in war-weary readers. Writing under the name "Petroleum V. Nasby," Locke used backwoods speech and spellings to tickle the public's funny bones. In one sketch, Nasby portrayed a draft-aged man anxious to stay out of the army: "My teeth is all unsound . . . and I hev hed bronkeetis 31 yeres last Joon . . . I hev korns and bunions on both feet which would prevent me from marchin."

No one was a bigger fan of humorists than the president of the United States. The day after the Union defeat at Fredericksburg, Illinois congressman Isaac N. Arnold dropped in at the White House to visit his harried friend. Lincoln began their conversation by reading aloud a selection by humorist Artemus Ward. When Lincoln laughed heartily afterward, Arnold was dumbfounded. "Is it possible," he asked the president, "that with the whole land bowed in sorrow . . . you can indulge in such levity?"

Lincoln abruptly threw down his book, tears streaming down his face. "If I could not get momentary respite from the crushing burden I am constantly carrying," he shot back, "my heart would break!"

Arnold left the Oval Office that afternoon with a new understanding of his president.

Opposite: A cartoonist pokes fun at Jefferson Davis.

PROTEST AND PEACE

They looked at one another,
and one of them did say,
'Twas never to join your army
we come to Amerikay.
To seek for bread and labor
as many's the man before,
And that's the only reason
we left the shamrock shore.
—Irish immigrant song

The Civil War did not always draw the people of a region together. Often, the clash of ideas on such issues as the draft, emancipation, and slavery bitterly divided the public, the press, and politicians alike. Draft-aged Northern whites were not always willing to risk death in battle to liberate Southern blacks in bondage. Irish and German immigrants who labored in Northern factories feared that freed blacks would compete with them for jobs and drive down wages. Midwestern farmers born in the South often sympathized with the struggles of the Confederacy.

On top of racial discord, the war brought financial hardship. To pay for armies and supplies, the Federal government created an income tax, the first in U.S. history. Next, the government squeezed out more revenues by levying taxes on liquor, tobacco, railroads, banks, and other sources.

As the war dragged on and casualties mounted, patience with the staggering cost wore thin. Politicians and newspapers grew louder in their criticism of the war. Frustrated citizens began taking their protests to the streets. Fearing that shrinking support for the war would hurt the Union's chances for success, the president was forced to take action.

As early as May 1861, Lincoln made his first move. Anxious to keep a rebellious Maryland from seceding, he dispatched troops under General Ben Butler to occupy the secessionist stronghold of Baltimore. Butler did not waste time holding a trial. Instead, he promptly threw the city's mayor and 19 secesh lawmakers into prison. Maryland took the hint and remained in the Union.

More drastic measures followed. To prevent spies from sending messages, Lincoln ordered many Northern telegraph offices seized. In selected areas, he suspended the writ of habeas corpus, which guarantees a citizen's right to a speedy trial. This action made it possible—if not quite legal—to keep suspected anti-Union agents in jail without a hearing.

Hostile Northern newspapers lashed back at Lincoln. "Half-witted," "incompetent," and "traitor" were just a few of the labels given him by angry journalists. In the case of the anti-Lincoln *Chicago Times,* the Lincoln administration had an effective way of dealing with the issue. The government simply shut down the paper.

Southward in Richmond, Lincoln's Rebel counterpart endured trials of his own. Formal, strong-willed, and determined, Jefferson Davis made a likely target for an often unfriendly press. Much of the criticism stemmed from the South's fear of a strong central government. Southerners believed that political power should rest with the individual states. But President Davis was directing a difficult, drawn-out war against a powerful enemy—the U.S. government. To win that war, he needed the same sweeping powers that Lincoln enjoyed. His efforts to muster this kind of authority brought down the anger of both politicians and newspapers. One Charleston newspaper sneeringly called Davis "this little head of a great country." The leading papers in Richmond, Raleigh, and

LINCOLN'S TWO DIFFICULTIES.

Lin. "WHAT? NO MONEY! NO MEN!"

Lincoln faced criticism at home and abroad. Here, the British magazine **Punch** *lampoons the president.*

Augusta attacked the Confederate president on a regular basis. Surprisingly, Davis made no attempt to muzzle the press that so often criticized him.

"RICH MAN'S WAR, POOR MAN'S FIGHT"

"July 14, 1863. . . . All day yesterday there were dreadful scenes enacted in the city. The police were successfully opposed; many were killed, many houses were gutted and burned. . . . All night long the fire-bells rang." So ran an account by Maria Lydig Daly of what some consider the most violent protest in U.S. history: the New York draft riots.

In few cities was the stage better set for a human explosion than New York. There, in its working-class neighborhoods, immigrant laborers sweated for low pay, fretted over war-spawned inflation, and bristled at the use of black workers to break labor strikes. And then there was the draft. Poor men could not afford to buy exemptions or hire substitutes. Muttering "rich man's war, poor man's fight," New York workers nursed their resentments until Monday, July 13, 1863.

At 9:00 A.M., a horde of club-wielding men and boys—mostly Irish immigrants—closed in on the draft office at Forty-sixth Street and Third Avenue. Inside, the government-ordered draft drawing was in full swing. The crowd flung a hail of stones, drove 60 policemen from the building, and set it ablaze. Now the destruction began in earnest.

The mob swept through the streets, beating a police superintendent and killing two members of the local Invalid Corps—a band of disabled veterans. Behind the male rioters came a gang of women and children. On Third Avenue, a crowd of more than 3,000 stormed the armory and sent it up in flames. Next, the Orphan Asylum of Colored Children on Fifth Avenue was ransacked and burned. Somehow, the 237 youngsters inside escaped unhurt. A black man in Greenwich Village was not so lucky. He was seized, strung up to a tree, and set afire.

The mobs also targeted newspapers that had favored the draft. The first floor of Horace Greeley's *Tribune* was totally destroyed. At the *Times*, editor Henry Raymond protected his building with the help of three Gatling guns on loan from the army.

All through the next two days, these "dreadful scenes" were repeated. It took the combined forces of five army regiments and volunteer crews to halt the violence. By Thursday, July 16, a fragile peace was restored to New York City. More than 100 people had died in the rioting. A month later, the draft drawing was continued. Ironically, only 12 percent of the men called up in that year's draft ever put on uniforms.

Three months earlier, J. B. Jones had been surprised to see "a few hundred women and boys" spilling into the streets of Richmond, Virginia. "About nine a.m., the mob emerged . . . and proceeded down Ninth Street," he wrote in his diary. "I asked a pale boy where they were going. A young woman . . . with a smile, answered that they were going to find something to eat."

They found it. Frustrated by soaring prices and worsening food shortages, the mostly female mob swarmed into Capitol Square. Their leader, a tall, pistol-brandishing woman named Mary Jackson, confronted Governor John Letcher with demands for fair food prices. The governor refused to cooperate. At this, the mob overran nearby stores, smashing windows and stealing food.

The rampage was brought to a climax by the arrival of armed Confederate troops. In the middle of the standoff, President Jefferson Davis appeared. Climbing onto a wagon, he faced the angry crowd. "You say you are hungry and have no money," he called out. "Here is all I have." With that, he flung out a handful of coins. Then he gave the mob five minutes to disperse. Warily eyeing the guns of the soldiers, the crowds melted away.

"A STAB IN THE DARK"

By the start of 1865, most Southerners knew time was running out for the Confederacy. The news from the battlefield was bleak. "We know that we have met with fearful reverses this year," a downhearted Kate Stone recorded in April. "Gallant old Charleston has fallen, Wilmington and Mobile have passed out of our hands, and . . . 'Brave Richmond on the James' has been taken." The specter of defeat haunted the war-weary population. Shortages, hunger, loss of loved ones, and the destruction of homes and property drained many Southern people of their determination and hope. "There is a gloom over all," Stone added, "like the shadow of Death." On April 9, the final blow fell. At Appomattox Court House, General Lee surrendered his hungry, exhausted army to Ulysses S. Grant.

Abraham Lincoln, at least to one Southerner, seemed the cause of all the South's misfortunes. "God," vowed the 26-year-old John Wilkes Booth, "made me the instrument of his punishment." On Good Friday evening, Booth slipped into the presidential box at Ford's Theater in Washington and fired one bullet into the back of Lincoln's head. Two weeks later, the young actor would be shot down outside a barn in Virginia.

While the Union mourned Lincoln's death, a manhunt began for John Wilkes Booth and his accomplices.

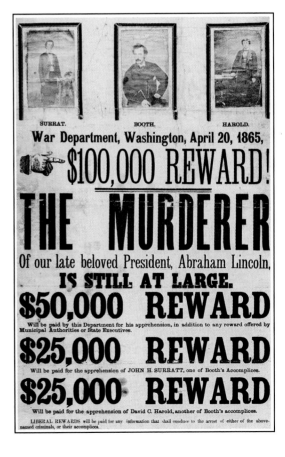

Lincoln was carried from the theater to a house across the street. There, he died just before 7:30 A.M. on April 15. Waves of shock and outrage rippled through the North. Calling his death a "dreadful tragedy," the *New York Times* praised Lincoln as "the head and hope . . . of the Republic." While Northerners and freed slaves mourned, many Confederates rejoiced. Others did not. Annie Harper realized that the North's loss was also the South's. "A brave people scorn a stab in the dark," she wrote. "Lincoln was a good man and the best friend of the southern people."

With the war over, the troubled Confederate government crumbled. Jefferson Davis was captured and thrown into a cell at Fortress Monroe, Virginia. There he stayed without trial for two years.

The devastation of the war was beyond anything Americans had ever seen. In four years of fighting, the factories and railroads of the South were nearly wiped out. Cities such as Atlanta, Charleston, and Richmond were left in smoking ruins. In state after state, homes and farms were ravaged and burned. All told, the Confederacy suffered $10 billion in ruined land and possessions. The loss of their slaves cost slaveholders a staggering $2 billion in lost "property."

In human terms, the destruction was even more frightening. After more than 10,000 battles, some 420,000 men from both regions returned home crippled or wounded. About 620,000 others never came back at all. "The dead, the dead, the dead," mourned Walt Whitman. "Our young men . . . taken from us—the son from the mother, the husband from the wife, the dear friend from the dear friend."

THE WAGES OF PEACE

For those who did return, homecoming was a happy, yet sometimes sobering, event. Rachel Cormany of Pennsylvania reacted this way to her reunion with her soldier-husband: "Joy to the world—*my* little world, at least. . . . *My* Precious is home safe from the war . . . now that [it] is over I hope we can once get to our own home and live as God intends we should." Private Leander Stilwell found little time for emotion when he reached his hometown of Otterville, Illinois, in the autumn of 1865:

My folks were expecting me . . . we all had a feeling of profound contentment and satisfaction . . . too deep to be expressed by mere words. I found that the farm work my father was then engaged in was cutting and shucking corn. So, the morning after my arrival, I . . . put on some of my father's old clothes and proceeded to wage war on the standing corn.

The end of the war brought a mixture of hope and fear for four million former slaves. Liberated from lives of bondage, many found the first days of freedom to be uncertain ones. One woman who had been a slave in Mississippi recorded her family's experience:

When freedom come, folks left home, out in the streets, crying, praying, singing, shouting, yelling and knocking down everything. Some shot off big guns. Then come the calm. It was sad then. So many folks done dead, things tore up, and nowheres to go. . . . Some folks starved nearly to death. Ma was a cripple woman. Pa couldn't find work for so long when he mustered out.

A Union soldier comes home.

A member of the Eighth Pennsylvania Volunteers displays his company's battle-torn flag one last time at war's end.

Thousands of newly freed blacks struck out on their own. Many others stayed with their former masters, working for pay or gradually buying small parcels of land to farm.

True freedom for black Americans was still a long way off. Slavery was officially abolished by passage of the Thirteenth Amendment in 1865. This act was soon followed by the Fourteenth and Fifteenth Amendments, which recognized blacks as U.S. citizens and gave black men the right to vote. But racial hatred could not be stamped out so easily. While blacks struggled to take their place in society, they were hampered by poverty and poor education. In Alabama, Tennessee, the Carolinas, and other states, they were hounded by extremist groups such as the Ku Klux Klan and the Knights of the White Camelia.

After the war, the North would ride the wave of its industrial might to greater prosperity. Meanwhile, the people of the South began a new struggle to rebuild their shattered economy and pride. The often harsh policies of Reconstruction—a process created by Northern politicians to control the Rebel states and restore them to the Union—would buffet the South for 12 years. The bitterness left by war and Reconstruction would linger for generations. "Of all the desolate conditions of the human heart," wrote Annie Harper, "few can compare with the feeling that you have no country, no flag, an exile in the land of your birth."

From the booming of the guns over Sumter to the crack of an assassin's pistol, the battles of the Civil War were over. But to the soldiers who fought them, a grim glory remained. "We have shared the incommunicable experience of war," wrote Union officer and future Supreme Court justice Oliver Wendell Holmes Jr. "We have felt . . . the passion of life to its top." Four years of hardship had deeply affected civilians, too. Recalling the start of the war, George Templeton Strong mused, "We have lived a century of common life since then." In an America that had changed forever, the years ahead would not be easy either.

SELECTED BIBLIOGRAPHY

Alcott, Louisa May. *Hospital Sketches.* New York: Sagamore Press, 1957.

Brooks, Stewart M. *Civil War Medicine.* Springfield, Ill.: C.C. Thomas, 1966.

Catton, Bruce. *The Civil War.* New York: The Fairfax Press, 1980.

Chang, Ina. *A Separate Battle: Women and the Civil War.* New York: Lodestar Books, 1991.

Channing, Steven A. *Confederate Ordeal: The Southern Home Front.* Alexandria, Va.: Time-Life Books, 1984.

Chesnut, Mary B. *Mary Chesnut's Civil War.* Edited by C. Vann Woodward. New Haven: Yale University Press, 1981.

Delbanco, Andrew. *The Portable Abraham Lincoln.* New York: Viking, 1992.

Douglass, Frederick. *Narrative of a Slave's Life.* Pathway Press, 1946.

Gragg, Rod. *The Illustrated Confederate Reader.* New York: Harper & Row, 1989.

Hamilton, Virginia. *Many Thousand Gone: African Americans from Slavery to Freedom.* New York: Alfred A. Knopf, 1993.

Harper, Annie Coulson. *Annie Harper's Journal: A Southern Mother's Legacy.* Edited by Jeannie Marie Deen. Corinth, Miss.: The General Store, 1992.

Hill, Lois. *Poems and Songs of the Civil War.* New York: The Fairfax Press, 1990.

Holmes, Sarah Katherine (Stone). *Brokenburn: The Journal of Kate Stone, 1861–1868.* Edited by John Q. Anderson. Baton Rouge: Louisiana State University Press, 1955.

Jackson, Donald Dale. *Twenty Million Yankees: The Northern Home Front.* Alexandria, Va.: Time-Life Books, 1985.

Jones, J. B. *A Rebel War Clerk's Diary, Vol. 2.* Philadelphia: J.B. Lippencott & Co., 1866.

Klein, Maury. *Life in Civil War America.* Harrisburg, Pa.: Historical Times, Inc. (Eastern Acorn Press), 1984.

McGuire, Judith W. *Diary of a Southern Refugee.* New York: Arno Press, 1972.

McPherson, James M. *Battle Cry of Freedom.* New York: Oxford University Press, 1988.

————. *Marching Toward Freedom: The Negro in the Civil War— 1861–1865.* New York: Alfred A. Knopf, 1965.

Meltzer, Milton. *Voices from the Civil War.* New York: Thomas Y. Crowell, 1989.

Meredith, Roy. *Mr. Lincoln's Cameraman: Mathew B. Brady.* New York: Dover Publications, Inc., 1974.

Miers, Earl Schenck and Richard A. Brown. *Gettysburg.* New York: Collier Books, 1962.

Mitgang, Herbert, ed. *Abraham Lincoln: A Press Portrait.* Chicago: Quadrangle Books, 1971.

Morgan, Sarah. *The Civil War Diary of a Southern Woman.* Edited by Charles East. New York: Touchstone Books, 1991.

Pember, Phoebe Yates. *A Southern Woman's Story.* Jackson, Tenn.: McCowat-Mercer Press, 1959.

Ray, Delia. *A Nation Torn.* New York: Lodestar Books, 1990.

Sandburg, Carl. *Abraham Lincoln: The Prairie Years and the War Years.* New York: Dell Publishing Co., Inc., 1974.

Stanchak, John E. *Leslie's Illustrated Civil War.* Jackson, Miss.: University Press of Mississippi, 1992.

Taft, Robert. *Photography and the American Scene: 1839–1889.* New York: Dover Publications, Inc., 1938.

Ward, Geoffrey C. *The Civil War.* New York: Alfred A. Knopf, 1990.

Whitman, Walt. *Portable Walt Whitman.* Edited by Mark Van Doren. New York: Viking, 1969.

Opposite: the ruins of Norfolk Navy Yard, 1864

INDEX

A newly freed drummer boy of the 78th Regiment, United States Colored Infantry

ACKNOWLEDGMENTS

Photographs and illustrations used with permission of the Library of Virginia: pp. 2, 15 (top and bottom), 66; the Bettmann Archive: pp. 6, 18, 33; Leib Image Archives: pp. 7, 8, 24, 31, 58; Library of Congress: pp. 10, 13, 28, 40, 42, 44, 48, 50, 60 (right), 62, 65, 68 (top), 70, 72, 74, 77, 79; Metropolitan Museum of Art, gift of Lyman C. Bloomingdale: p. 11; UPI/Bettmann: pp. 16, 20; Valentine Museum, Richmond, Va.: p. 17; Harriet Beecher Stowe Center, Hartford, Conn.: p. 27; Independent Picture Service: pp. 21, 22, 57; National Archives: pp. 32, 34, 41, 43, 53, 54, 55, 63, 80, 84, 88; Atlanta Historical Society: p. 35; Historic Northampton, Northampton, Mass.: p. 36; Old Court House Collection, Vicksburg, Miss.: p. 38; Chicago Historical Society: pp. 47, 68 (bottom); Drake Well Museum, Titusville, Pa.: p. 52; American Red Cross: p. 60 (left).

Front cover: Library of Congress
Back cover: Indianapolis Museum of Art, James E. Roberts Fund

DEC   1996